Jesus On The Trainline

JESUS *ON THE* TRAINLINE

Tell Him what you Want

BEVERLY WEIR

XULON PRESS

Xulon Press
555 Winderley Pl, Suite 225
Maitland, FL 32751
407.339.4217
www.xulonpress.com

Paperback ISBN-13: 978-1-66288-508-2
Ebook ISBN-13: 978-1-66288-509-9

Dedication

This book is dedicated to people who like to think "out of the box" when it comes to their faith in God; people who have the desire to take the limits off God and get a glimpse of Him in their everyday lives. Because in Matthew 28:20, Jesus said, "I am with you always [remaining with you perpetually—regardless of circumstance, and on every occasion], even to the end of the age."

When Jesus said He is with us "always," He did not mean only on Sundays or in church. He is with us now!

Acknowledgements

First and always, all thanks go to my Lord and Savior, Jesus Christ. Without God's Holy Spirit prompting me to author this book, it would not have been written.

A sincere thank you to my husband for his love, support, and patience; the man who gives me a boost of confidence when I need it.

Special thanks to the godly women in my life. You know who you are; the ones who texted and called me and provided the encouragement I needed to pursue what God placed in my heart to do.

A huge thanks and much love to my parents. I thank God for both of you every day and am so grateful to have you in my life.

DISCLAIMER: The train experiences in this book are from the author. This is not to promote riding on any trains or indicating that God is only on trains. The author is sharing her experience and would like to express the importance of not putting God "in a box" and not limiting where or how God might speak to you.

Table of Contents

Prologue

Hearing and singing gospel songs brought joy to my heart. There was a message in the music that would meet my need or answer a certain question that was plaguing my mind. There was confirmation in the lyrics. Amazingly, the words to a specific gospel song I was listening to seemed to speak to me about where I was spiritually in my relationship with God and others. Surprisingly, the song also provided directions or instructions on what I needed to do next. It was interesting that some lyrics would provide guidance on if I needed to resolve an issue, repent, or reevaluate a situation. I believe that the Lord sometimes would place songs on my heart to share with others to meet their needs. Oftentimes, the words to some songs gave me a sense of peace. Whether the song spoke to me about the mercies of God or His promises, the music calmed my soul.

Lastly, I noticed that the words to some songs gave me new revelations about who I am as a child of God.

There are lessons in the lyrics.

On March 17, 2023, the Lord placed a song on my heart. I woke up singing the song "Power of Your Love."[1] The songwriter is Geoff Bullock, and the music was recorded by Hillsong Worship.

What an awesome song to wake up to! It was declaring my desire for God to be closer, and I believe the Lord was speaking to me through this song. When I listen to it, I recall Isaiah 40:31, *But those who wait on the Lord shall renew their strength; They shall mount up with wings like eagles, They shall run and not be weary, They shall walk and not faint.* This Bible verse gave me the direction that I am to wait on the Lord. This was the position I needed to take in this circumstance. There was a decision that needed to be made for my family's future. I did not know the direction I should take because it involved a substantial change in my life. There are times when God wants you to take a leap of faith, and there are times when He wants you to wait. This was a clear indication for me to wait. As mentioned, this is how God speaks to me. I believe every child of God hears and sees God based on their relationship with Him. I cannot say my way is the only way, nor can we dismiss how God speaks to others, but if the direction or instruction aligns with God's Word, His promises for His people, and His character, perhaps it is just how God speaks to you.

Maybe I am speaking for myself, but I know God is here and closer than we think. My desire is to be closer to God and for Him to show me His love. Circumstances in life can bring wounds to the heart, and we want to get into the presence of God where there is healing, comforting peace, and a realization that God absolutely loves us.

Furthermore, other lyrics to the song brought me to not only Isaiah 40:31, but also to Psalm 27:14, *Wait on the Lord; Be of good courage, And He shall strengthen your heart; Wait, I say, on the Lord!* My message from the Lord that day was to wait on Him. Instead of taking matters into my own hands, I am to rely on and expect to see God move in the circumstance and give me direction.

I am so glad God can use anything and anyone to speak to us. As I sang this song, the words covered me with peace. Just knowing God's love surrounds us brings us so much joy and confidence!

Some history on March 17. It is the day that Irish Americans celebrate Saint Patrick's Day. Also, it commemorates the day in 1992 that ended apartheid. Shannon Jacobs's article titled "Number 17 Meaning In The Bible And Its Significance To Us" provides a biblical perspective of this number.

In the Bible, the number seventeen symbolizes "overcoming the adversary" and "full victory." On the seventeenth day of the Hebrew month, when God started to flood the land with rain, He conquered the sins of disobedient mankind.

Right in the heart of God's annual holy season known as the Feast of Tabernacles, Noah's ark and its eight occupants came to rest on the seventeenth of the seventh month. On top of that, the heavenly Father raised Jesus Christ from the dead shortly before sundown on 17 Nisan, giving him total victory and triumph over the grave and death.[4]

I am waiting and expecting to see God's "full victory" in my life!

Preface

How It Started

Becoming an author was not on my list of "what I want to be when I grow up." It came naturally. When I was younger, I enjoyed writing in my journal. It was my way of expressing my feelings. Sometimes, I wrote poetry and songs, but the thought of writing books never crossed my mind. But God had a plan. Although writing brought me joy, it was not until a certain instance that made me feel as if my heart was broken beyond repair—one of my aunts passed away. At that moment in time, God stepped in. Through the brokenness and pain, God spoke to me and said, *"Write about it."* I believe God brought forth and refined this hidden talent. What flowed out were words that helped to release the pain. My God-given talent and abilities were released, and I believe God wants me to share the experiences of how He is alive and intervening in the world with others. Also, I recall when the Lord spoke to my heart and said, *"Feed My sheep."* I believe my books and other written materials are how I can do what God called me to do—feed His sheep.

As I wrote this book, the title that came to mind was *Jesus on the Trainline—Tell Him What You Want.* I couldn't help but laugh. When I told my husband the title of my next book, he laughed as did one of my dearest friends when I told her.

There are times in the Bible when God revealed a promise and others laughed. For example:

> *Then Abraham fell on his face and laughed, and said in his heart, "Shall a child be born to a man who is one hundred years old? And shall Sarah, who is ninety years old, bear a child?"* Genesis 17:17

> *Therefore, Sarah laughed within herself, saying, "After I have grown old, shall I have pleasure, my lord being old also?"* Genesis 18:12

Yes, I, too, thought the title *Jesus on the Trainline—Tell Him What You Want* was quite funny. I truly believe God has a sense of humor. Perhaps some of you might recall the song "Jesus on the Main Line (Tell Him What You Want)." It was written by Fred Mc Dowell and sung by various Christian artists and many church choirs. From confirmation to revelation, I had many of my concerns and prayers answered while just commuting to and from work, events, or other activities on the subway train. The reason for the title is because I never imagined that as I meditated on God's Word and inwardly spoke to Him, He would reveal Himself to me on a train. Yes, I know God is omnipresent, but on the train was not one of the places I would imagine He would speak to me or my situation! In my book *Vessels of Honor,*[2] I wrote about how God, for the first time, revealed an answer to my question on the train. It is in the chapter titled "Seal of Approval."

We know that God is omnipresent, and with that knowledge, why wouldn't His presence be on the train? God appears in places where we need Him, and He could send His angels on our behalf. In Daniel 3, Jesus appeared in the fiery furnace with Shadrach, Meshach, and Abed-Nego. In Daniel 6, He sent His angels in the den of lions.

I believe that after reading *Jesus on the Trainline—Tell Him What You Want,* you will never look at your commute on public transportation the same. This is not a remedy or ritual to follow. I am sharing my experiences on how God met me and answered my prayers. Everyone's relationship with God is different; however, you never know if God will answer your prayers outside of a normal environment. Also, the brief history of the lettered trainlines is something that you may not know about; specifically, how these trainlines were started. Nonetheless, the next time you're on the train, bus, cab, or car, you may be surprised that God can, indeed, answer your prayers.

Let the words of my mouth and the meditation of my heart Be acceptable in Your sight, O Lord, my strength and my Redeemer. Psalm 19:14

Introduction

The New York City Train

Born and raised in New York, I enjoyed the "city that never sleeps." Prior to the pandemic, I enjoyed taking the train to see on and off-Broadway theatre plays and movies and eat at some of the tastiest restaurants in the city. I love French cuisine, and one of my favorite restaurants is Chez Josephine. I would also visit museums and attend other events to expand my knowledge and understanding of other cultures. I loved taking the train to the Museum of Modern Art, Met Cloisters, or the Guggenheim. I do not know why, but I was fascinated with other cultures and foods. I am in awe at God's creation; it is amazing to see the beauty and variety presented in the world. From the different colored flowers, animals, and people to the aromatic and delicious drinks and foods, all are unique and display His creative attributes and how we should respect and not abuse any of God's creations.

When Rudy Giuliani was mayor, I saw 42nd Street transform to a more family-oriented entertainment and activities. While working at a company located on 47th Street in Manhattan before this transformation, I was concerned about leaving the office late because I needed to walk to the 42nd Street station to catch the train to go home. The streets were filthy with trash and debris and there was crime. God does protect us, but He has also given us common sense not to go anywhere or do anything that would cause us harm.

There was a time when I thought going to a concert was innocent. Once when I went to go see one of my favorite performers, a pop culture singer, I could feel a heaviness in my spirit. It felt as if my body wanted to make a U-turn to not go to the concert. The excitement I felt weeks before attending the concert seemed to vanish as I entered Madison Square Garden. Unbeknownst to me, there was unseen danger. For some reason, my spirit man did not receive the songs and performance. As I sat there, I felt uncomfortable and wanted to get up and leave, but I stayed with my friend. If you feel uncomfortable about a person or place, do not dismiss the feeling. There was no physical danger; the danger was spiritual. The lyrics to the music and the way the performer danced was displeasing to me. It was unusual because before, I enjoyed this performer, but now, it seemed wrong to watch and hear this entertainer. I do not know if it was God developing my discernment. All I knew was that I was not pleasing God by being there. I had to repent of my disobedience to the prompting of the Holy Spirit. We are not God. We do not know everything. There are times when you need to withdraw from certain places for your protection. Gary Thomas once said, "On still other occasions, He [Jesus] retreated for His own refreshment and renewal or protection." Even Jesus withdrew and did not go places in order to protect Himself.

We read many times in the Bible that Jesus withdrew from the crowd. Matthew 12:14 is one example: *Then the Pharisees went out and plotted against Him [Jesus], how they might destroy Him. But when Jesus knew it, He withdrew from there.* Do not ignore those promptings from the Holy Spirit when you are traveling in a crowd or just in general. I must admit I have ignored some and wished I had not. I cannot change the past, but I can ask God for forgiveness. Thank you, God, for Your mercy and grace! Nonetheless, I thank

God for His protection throughout the years and even now. Overall, the transformation from 42nd Street from then to now was amazing.

As mentioned, the New York City train was the mode of transportation I took to get to these destinations. Interestingly, the extreme contrast of activities on the subway that occurred ranged from unique entertainment, "right on time" inspiration to, unfortunately, petty crimes. I recall the young men who would do acrobatic stunts using the poles in the subway car to perform feats of tumbling and twirls as the train moved through the tunnel. There were also the people who brought ministry on the trains, declaring to others that Jesus is the only one who saves.

Sometimes, entering the train brought a horrific scent from the homeless people who slept on the seats as a warm place to lay their heads. The sound of music filled the air as musicians sang or played instruments. You might pick up a piece of art that was displayed on the platform. There was underground entertainment and shopping. In general, the subway harbored the good and the bad. Some trains moved through the dark tunnel with rapid speed while others moved at a slower pace. If you were looking through the window of the first subway car, you could see the bright light as it traveled outside. Sometimes the glaring light would hurt your eyes, but it was a sign that you were coming out. It was the picture of the light at the end of the tunnel. There is a beginning to an end, and the revelation of your coming out was a subtle reminder that there is hope in any situation with the Lord.

I recall the times I would enter the subway with the sunlight in the sky to exit at my stop when the sun had set. Daylight savings time in the United States gave me the opportunity to see more sunlight in the spring and summer months. In my opinion, it was amazing to see that there was still sunlight when exiting the train. I had good and very few bad experiences with this mode of transportation we call the New York City Transit.

God Does Speak

You need to personally know and hear God in the journey of establishing a relationship with the Creator of this universe; however, to understand when God is speaking is a true blessing. I knew God through the words of family as well as through the ministers and pastors of our home church. It was a tradition to go to church every Sunday. Often, it was a time to dress up and look our best. The words spoken during the sermons were inspiring, and I strongly believe my family believed in Proverbs 22:6, *Train up a child in the way he should go and when he is old, he will not depart.* That training was a part of me beginning the journey to find God, or as they say, "know Him for yourself." According to Isaiah 55:6 (NIV), we are to "seek the LORD while he may be found; call on him while he is near." Psalm 34:18 tells us that "the Lord is close to the brokenhearted and saves those who are crushed in spirit."

The fellowship and gatherings were enlightening and provided a foundation for my spiritual growth that I would need as I matured in faith. During my younger years and as I was being exposed to the church environment, the foundation was established. Some planted or said encouraging words from the Bible or spoke about God's goodness while others watered by reinforcing my knowledge of God's goodness and promises, but there was no increase. I had not yet allowed the faith of God to penetrate my heart or life to fully believe He was, indeed, God! I had allowed the cares of life to become bigger than my God. As Jesus said in Matthew 13:8:

Some fell on stony places, where they did not have much earth; and they immediately sprang up because they had no depth of earth. But when the sun was up they were scorched, and because they had no root they withered away. And some fell among thorns, and the thorns sprang up and choked them. But others fell on good ground and yielded a crop: some a hundredfold, some sixty, some thirty.

I had a foundation in God's Word, but the worries of the world had made me stagnant. My young roots needed watering so they could grow deeper. I needed to trust in God regardless of the circumstances so I would have a solid rock foundation. As mentioned, Matthew 7:24-25 tell us,

"Therefore whoever hears these sayings of Mine [Jesus], and does them, I will liken him to a wise man who built his house on the rock: and the rain descended, the floods came, and the winds blew and beat on that house; and it did not fall, for it was founded on the rock." Building a strong foundation requires not only hearing God's commands, but also *obeying* them.

Jesus on the Trainline

Little did I know my adventures on the New York City train would be my training ground for God to answer my questions and educate me on what I needed and did not need to do. Yes, the subway is one of the places where God trained me and began to build my foundation in Jesus Christ.

The New York Mass Transit is remarkably interesting. Prior to the pandemic, the connections and terminals showed the creative style of people. There were artists, musicians, and other entertainment on these subways. You would see food or merchandise vendors. I also recall the women who walked along the subway platforms selling churros. On hot days, you could see people selling cold bottled water that they kept in a rolling cooler or shopping cart. You might have also seen young children selling boxed chocolates or candies on the train to support their school's sports team or event. More exciting was you might hear a friend or neighbor calling out to you and waving across the platform. The most interesting time, which I call "divine intervention," is when God places you on the right train at the right time to speak a word in season to a friend or neighbor. It is amazing!

At this time, I lived in Brooklyn, New York. I would take the train to Manhattan, Queens, and the Bronx on various occasions; however, my normal subway commute to work was to Manhattan. I mainly rode the L train and sometimes transferred to the A and then D or F trains. There were also numbered trains I rode, but for this book, we will focus mainly on the "lettered" trains.

Background on the New York City Trainlines

A little history on the subway system in New York:

- "The New York Subway opened in 1904 and is the state's longest metro system and one of the world's largest underground lines. It has nearly 500 stations and a total of 660 miles of tracks (1,060 km)."[5]
- "Oct. 27, 1904 — 150,000 people rode the subway when it opened to the public for the first time, regarding the new form of public transit more as a circus act than as part of the drudgery of daily life."[6]
- "2019 ridership, Average weekday subway ridership: 5.5 million. There are 15 lettered routes, not including shuttle service: A, B, C, D, E, F, G, J, L, M, N, Q, R, W, Z."[7]

Wow, from 150,000 in 1904 people to 5.5 million in 2019; that's a lot of people riding the trains. I can recall the days when I would think to myself while riding on the train during rush hour, *We look like sardines in a can in these subway cars*. However, the number of passengers dwindled during COVID-19. Fewer people were riding the trains. In fact:

For the first time in its 115-year history, the entire New York City subway system was intentionally shut down on Wednesday [May 6, 2020]. The famed train system is one of only a handful in the country that usually runs 24 hours a day; however, as the pandemic grips the city, the Metropolitan Transportation Authority has decided it would be best to suspend service from 1 a.m. to 5 a.m. to disinfect the entire system in hopes of slowing the spread of the virus, The New York Times reports. Since March, ridership has fallen by over 90 percent.[8]

A horrific and heartbreaking time in history for not only New York, but for the world. I have close family and friends who got sick from COVID-19, and thank God, they recovered. Unfortunately, there were a few who passed away because of the virus. I recall during this dreadful time when COVID-19 cases were high and there was no vaccine, God placed on my heart that Psalm 91 was the reverse of the virus. Psalm 91 was a prayer of protection. It is a psalm I read daily. As mentioned, there is no special formula or method for being protected from the circumstances or challenges in life, but there is hope and trust in God to protect His people. It was a time to seek God's face and ask for His help. According to 2 Chronicles 7:14, the Lord said, *If My people who are called by My name will humble themselves, and pray and seek My face, and turn from their wicked ways, then I will hear from heaven, and will forgive their sin and heal their land.* We need our land to be healed by God!

Considering most of the world is slowly recovering from a "shutdown," we are not doing business as usual. During this time in history, there was a shift, in my opinion, from self-serving to serving others, especially for those who are in the roles of first responders. God, continue to bless and keep the first responders. Those who are first responders, we appreciate all the work you have done. You are valued and honored so much for all of your sacrifices and help.

Jesus Christ wants His church to have a serving attitude and to be servants of God. We need first responders in the faith—men and women who are called to do the work of the ministry; those who are appointed by God to provide what this lost world needs—to accept Jesus as their Lord and Savior. Those who are doers of the Word and not hearers only (James 1:22). Also, godly men and women who know, preach, and teach of God's true grace of salvation: *For certain people have crept in unnoticed [just as if they were sneaking in by a side door]. They are ungodly persons whose condemnation was predicted long ago, for they distort the grace of our God into decadence and immoral freedom [viewing it as an opportunity to do whatever they want], and deny and disown our only Master and Lord, Jesus Christ* (Jude 1:4 AMP). As it is stated in the Lord's Prayer, *not my will, but Your will be done*, doing the things God wants us to do and not satisfying our selfish desires.

"A" Train

Whether you are riding a particular train or remember the train or trains you rode, imagine that the letter of the subway line represents a promise or hope from God. If you're not a train rider, here are some things you might think about when it comes to subway lines or trains.

"Opened in 1932, the A-train is the longest route in the New York City Subway System. At a whopping 31 miles, the A-train stretches all the way from Inwood in northern Manhattan to the Rockaways and Richmond Hill in southeastern Queens". Unlike other lines in the system, the A-train has four separate termini, with each acting as the gateway to four distinct neighborhoods.[9]

If you happen to ride this train during your daily commute, you could read your Bible and start reading the books in the Bible that begin with "A." Yes, it might seem like a simple way to begin, and one might say, "Is this the only extent of your Bible reading?" Of course not. This is just one way of getting into the habit of reading the Bible. Why not discuss with your family or friends about what books in the Bible begin with the letter "A"? In fact, Amos and Acts are two books out of the sixty-six books in the Bible that begin with "A." You could engage in God's words from the Old and the New Testaments respectively. Most importantly, let God meet you in His Word.

Also, you could meditate on how awesome (another word that begins with "A") God is and even search through Scripture for words beginning with "A" that show positive affirmation of the goodness of God. In Daniel 7, you could get more acquainted with the "Ancient of Days." Daniel spoke of his vision in this chapter, and in verse 9, he describes what he saw in his vision: *"I watched till thrones were put in place, And the Ancient of Days was seated; His garment was white as snow, And the hair of His head was like pure wool. His throne was a fiery flame, Its wheels a burning fire."* Our God is seated on the throne with all power and authority. He is an awesome God!

Yes, the A train reminds me of how "awesome" God is. Reflecting on Daniel 9:4, it reads, *And I prayed to the Lord my God, and made confession, and said, "O Lord, great and awesome God, who keeps His covenant and mercy with those who love Him, and with those who keep His commandments."* The A train that you take on your normal routine subway ride (or if you are just discovering this train) gives you an opportunity to read your Bible and declare God's promises.

Not only were my prayers or questions answered during my commute, but I would also receive corrections. I recall while sitting on a seat on a subway train, a woman sat next to me. Although this woman reeked of cigarette smoke, I never verbally expressed my discontent. I was uncomfortable smelling it because I am not a smoker. Sometimes, you smell the perfume or cologne of passengers, even the aroma of coffee. You could also smell those who perhaps forgot to put on deodorant. It was a part of the air we breathed on the subway. As I smelled the cigarette smoke, I was looking for another seat to sit in so I could avoid the smell. It was a crowded train, and there was nowhere else to sit. I was disappointed because I had a long way to ride on this train, and most likely, this woman was not getting off the train until we reached Manhattan (we were still in Brooklyn). I believe God was checking my attitude. If so, I failed. I must admit I was complaining in my mind about the cigarette smell that this woman carried. Then, as if she was reading my mind, she apologized to me. Perhaps, she saw the disguised disgust on my face. Only God knows, but she said, "Sorry about the smell of smoke. I am a heavy smoker, and I just can't seem to quit." Whoa, God convicted me! I said it was okay and mentioned for her to ask God to help her. Cigarette smoking was her heavy load or burden.

I had to apologize to God, and although I was uncomfortable smelling the lingering odor of cigarette smoke, her words changed my perspective. I no longer focused or complained about the smell of cigarette smoke. Yes, my perspective had changed; now, I was praying or asking God to help her with her struggle and desire to quit smoking. You never know if those chance meetings are ways for God to check your attitude or an opportunity to minister to someone. Also, I realized that habits do control the will of some people. Just because they do it does not mean they like doing it. It is a habit that needs breaking. Some people are not strong enough to break a habit. It is a burden to them and perhaps their family; however, we have a burden barrier. Jesus said, *"Take My yoke upon you and learn from Me, for I am gentle and lowly in heart, and you will find rest for your souls. For My yoke is easy and My burden is light"* (Matt. 11:29-30). And according to Mark 10:27, *But Jesus looked at them and said, "With men it is impossible, but not with God; for with God all things are possible."* Jesus can break any habit! As I read the word "impossible," I think of the great I AM, the one who makes things possible. In Exodus 3:14, the great I AM appeared to Moses: *And God said to Moses, "I AM WHO I AM." And He said, "Thus you shall say to the children of Israel, 'I AM has sent me to you.'"* I can imagine God saying, "I AM the one who heals, I AM the one who delivers, I AM the one who saves, I AM the one who provides, I AM your peace, I AM the one who can help you break that habit," and the list can go on and on because the great I AM is in control.

From convictions to revelations, riding the train was a learning experience about the great I AM for me.

O Lord, great and awesome God, who keeps His covenant and mercy with those who love Him. Daniel 9:4

“B” Train

The names IRT, BMT, and IND were the names of the three competing transit agencies prior to city takeover in the 40s. The Independent Subway (IND) was formed by the City in the 1920s as an “independent” system that was not connected to the IRT or BMT lines ... The IND lines were the 8th Avenue and 6th Avenue trunk lines in Manhattan, the Queens Boulevard subway in Queens, the Concourse subway in the Bronx, the Fulton Street subway in Brooklyn, the Brooklyn/Queens Crosstown, and the line in Brooklyn via Smith/9th Sts. To Church Avenue ... After city takeover of the bankrupt BMT and IRT companies on June 1, 1940, many of the elevated lines were closed, and a slow “unification” took place ... The Chrystie Street connection in Manhattan, which opened in November, 1967, unified the Manhattan Bridge lines of the BMT with the Sixth Avenue lines of the IND, such that trains from Brooklyn now had access to all the BMT and IND trunk lines in Manhattan (6th, 8th, Broadway, and Nassau St.).[7 10]

Until November 1967, the B train ran on the sixth avenue line, but it exclusively ran in Manhattan. "Exclusively" reminds me of God's promise that we are a royal priesthood. According to 1 Peter 2:9, *But you are a chosen generation, a royal priesthood, a holy nation, His own special people, that you may proclaim the praises of Him who called you out of darkness into His marvelous light, who once were not a people but are now the people of God, who had not obtained mercy but now have obtained mercy.*

Royalty is exclusivity.

Back to the letter "B." Words like "blessed" and "believe" come to mind. This could be a time when you think about how blessed you are. Oftentimes, we focus on the negative, but think about how good God is and has been. Thank Him for what He has brought you through and praise Him for what He is about to do. Those little blessings that you might think are nothing to you could mean a great deal to someone else. We tend to think our situation is hopeless and minimize anyone's feelings or thoughts; however, if we take time and think about others' situations, just by reading or watching the news, I am sure you will be grateful for where you are and what you have.

You are blessed if you have health and strength, no mental issues ("a right mind"), a place to call your own, food to eat, clean water, clothes to wear, shoes on your feet, your children are healthy and doing well, income coming in, and I am sure you can think of other people or things that you are grateful and thankful for that God has provided for or is consistently giving you. There is hope in God for He is Jehovah-Jira, our Provider! Some of these things some people take for granted, but they mean a lot, and you ought to thank God for them! You should be grateful that God is providing for your every need! In general, the people and things we take for granted are the people and things we should be grateful and thankful for. Just think about them and know that you are truly blessed and highly favored by God.

I recall I was on the train heading to work, and most of the time, if I was in the first subway car, I liked to stand by the subway car window and watch as the train traveled down the tunnel. Yes, I was like a kid looking out the window as if I was on some amusement park ride. I would watch as the train went around the curves and entered the stations. When the train elevated from the lower level to the higher level or vice versa, it was almost like a rollercoaster ride without the steep slopes. There was an underground traffic light system like the one above ground that directed train traffic.

One day, while on the train, somehow the latch that held the subway door unlocked. When the train made a sharp turn, I watched as the door flung completely open. If you are familiar with how subway cars are connected, there are connecting cars with doors in front and back. There are gaps between each car that some people would open the door to travel to the next car. It so happened that the door in the front of the train that should have been locked was now unlocked. I could see the train tracks clearly as the train moved down the tunnel. With the door now opened, the debris that was on the subway tracks was flying into the subway car. Paper, food wrappers, and cups that had been thrown on the subway tracks were now twirling like a whirlwind into the subway car (those who throw trash on the subway tracks should be ashamed). Luckily, the conductor responded by shutting the door and securing it with a stick to prevent the door from reopening. It was a scary scene; thank God, I had not stood in that area as I quite often did when I was in the first subway car. Only God knows what could have happened if I had been standing there when the door flung open.

I believe in divine intervention. I heard stories of how God or His angels have stepped in at the right time or moment to save a person. I think others can also attest that they plan to do one thing, and for some reason, they decide to do something else. As Proverbs 3:5-6 says, *Trust in the Lord with all your heart And lean not on your own understanding; In all your ways acknowledge Him, And He shall direct your paths.* When a thought comes to mind to deviate from your plan, heed the warning. I believe it is God directing your steps. Thank God for His mercy and grace and that no one got hurt. Perhaps you can think of a time when you could not explain how something happened, but you knew if you were there, you could have experienced harm. All you could say was that it was divine intervention or the hand of God.

To believe in God is to have trust in Him. According to John 12:46 (AMP), Jesus said, *I have come as Light into the world, so that everyone who believes and trusts in Me [as Savior—all those who anchor their hope in Me and rely on the truth of My message] will not continue to live in darkness.*

As you ride through that dark tunnel on the train, you know that soon you will see the light. When the train comes out of the dark tunnel, there is a sense of a breakthrough. We have a promise from God that Jesus is the Light of the World. He brings hope to dark situations. He is our breakthrough for every circumstance and situation in our lives.

As Walter Hawkins said in his song, "Be grateful." We can also be thankful, be forgiving, be hopeful, be joyful, and be loving, just to name a few. My question to you is, what is your positive "B" or "be"?

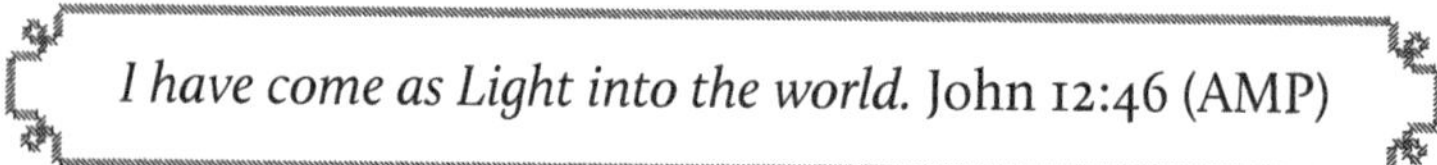
I have come as Light into the world. John 12:46 (AMP)

"C" Train

This train also runs on the eighth avenue line; however, when compared to the A train, it runs locally. Sometimes, we need to slow down and take time to hear clearly from God. If your commute includes the C train and you are on this train for longer than three stops before you reach your destination, perhaps this could be the time you could spend reading chapters and verses that start with the letter "C." From 1 and 2 Chronicles, 1 and 2 Corinthians, and Colossians, I truly believe God's Word will penetrate your mind and heart during these times.

Short train rides could represent times to slow down and focus on the people that God has placed in your life. Sometimes, with the hurrying here and there, we tend to neglect ourselves and others. This is not intentional. It relates to our busy lives, especially if we have more obligations than time to do them. Think of hobbies or activities you used to enjoy doing. When was the last time you rode a bike, painted a picture, planted a seed, looked up at the sky, pampered yourself, or complimented others or yourself, just to name a few?

There are also simple ways to show someone you care. It could be as simple as cooking their favorite meal, picking up something they need from the store, calling to say hi, texting an encouraging word, or whatever the Lord places on your heart to do. Self-care is important, too. Take a moment to relax your mind and think of the goodness of God.

I recall one day the Lord placed on my heart to send someone flowers. The thought came to mind and it would not go away until I sent the flowers. To my surprise, the person was so grateful for the flowers and explained to me that she was having an exhausting day, and the flowers were a pleasant surprise. I did not know the reason why God pressed upon my heart to send the flowers, but God knew it would cheer her up. Be obedient to God when He speaks.

Showing compassion and concern for others is not a sign of weakness. As followers of Christ, we take on the same characteristics of God. Psalm 145:8 reminds us that "the Lord is gracious and full of compassion, Slow to anger and great in mercy." Throughout His walk here on Earth, Jesus showed compassion for others. As He hung on the cross, we read about His compassion and concern for others. He told one disciple to care for His mother. He was not only focused on His current situation, but He also had compassion and thought about the needs of others.

With all of the pain Jesus went through from being beaten by the Roman guards, getting pierced in His hands and feet, to hanging on the cross, He focused on the needs of others. Sometimes, through heavy storms or challenges in life, we can take time to help or pray for others. You perhaps read or heard about the story of Job. He was a faithful man, and God allowed Satan to test him. We all have our own tests that God allows for a reason to mature us and improve our character. The test may be different, but the purpose is designed specifically for the individual. There are no two people who are alike. Even identical twins are unique. Psalms 139:13-14 tells us, *For you created my innermost being; you knit me together in my mother's womb. I praise you because I am fearfully and wonderfully made; your works are wonderful.* I know that full well; however, there is one thing I believe God was teaching us through the story of Job. It is in Job 42:10: *And the Lord restored Job's losses when he prayed for his friends.* Indeed, the Lord gave Job twice as much as he had before when he took the focus off of himself and prayed for others. We see that God restored the lost.

Jesus did not focus only on what He was going through while He was on the cross. He was not oblivious to or denied the fact that there were things that needed to be taken care of.

> John 19:26-27 (NKJV) says, *When Jesus therefore saw His mother, and the disciple whom He loved standing by, He said to His mother, "Woman, behold your son!" Then He said to the disciple, "Behold your mother!" And from that hour that disciple took her to his own home.*

A simple text or call to say hi or to see if everything is okay are just a couple of ways you can, for the moment, take the focus off of your concerns and focus on others. I know that my life is full of things I need to do, but I do try to take time to hear from God's Holy Spirit who leads me and guides me into all truth. As mentioned before, I am not perfect, but I am learning to become more aware of God's still, small voice of instruction or direction on what I need to do for others and what to take care of during the challenges of life.

The Lord is gracious and full of compassion, slow to anger and great in mercy. Psalm 145:8

"D" Train

The D train service began on December 15, 1940, when the IND Sixth Avenue Line openedThe D train Sixth Avenue Express is a rapid transit service of the New York City Subway. The D train is colored bright orange on route signs, station signs, and the official subway map since it uses the IND Sixth Avenue Line through Manhattan ... The D train service operates at all times between 205th Street in Norwood, Bronx, and Stillwell Avenue in Coney Island, Brooklyn via Concourse in the Bronx, Eighth Avenue (under Central Park West) and Sixth Avenue in Manhattan, and the north side of the Manhattan Bridge to and from Brooklyn. In Brooklyn, D train service operates via the BMT Fourth Avenue and West End lines. It is the only B Division service to operate full time in the Bronx.[11]

Coney Island was a place we would go to as children. I remember riding the D or F train to the beach. My friends and I were young. I did not know how to swim at the time, but I loved standing at the shore just to get my feet wet. In fact, before getting our feet wet, we would run from the waves as they got closer and closer to our feet. It was a game to outrun the wave. The water was cold, and perhaps unknowingly, it was our way of prepping ourselves before getting into the cold water. I was adventurous (I guess like all kids who have little fear) on that sunny and sweltering day at the beach. I went from running from the waves to jumping into one. Even though I did not know how to swim, I was told that the wave would bring me back to the shore. With this thought in my mind, I made the leap. It was not a leap of faith, but a leap of grace. Now, I can imagine that God was saying, *"This girl does not know what she is doing."* I went down in the water and the wave took me back to the shore, but it was not as quick as I anticipated. I held my breath, but could not hold it long enough. By the time I was able to walk out of the ocean, I had swallowed some seawater. It was by the grace of God that I did not drown, though I am quite sure one of the lifeguards would have spotted me if there was dire danger. The thought if that was one of the times when God saved me returned years later because as I got older, I heard of waves that brought people out to sea and they drowned, but my wave brought me back to safety because God had a plan for my life. God said in Jeremiah 29:11, *For I know the thoughts that I think toward you, says the Lord, thoughts of peace and not of evil, to give you a future and a hope.*

If your commute is from Brooklyn to the Bronx and the train you ride is the D, you're in for a delightful time in the Word of God. There are two books in the Bible that begin with the letter "D." They are Deuteronomy and Daniel. Also, you could read about the life of David in 1 Samuel, how God choose a young shepherd boy to be anointed and become the king of Israel. In 1 Samuel 16:1-7, we read:

> *Now the Lord said to Samuel, "How long will you mourn for Saul, seeing I have rejected him from reigning over Israel? Fill your horn with oil and go; I am sending you to Jesse the Bethlehemite. For I have provided Myself a king among his sons." And Samuel said, "How can I go? If Saul hears it, he will kill me." But the Lord said, "Take a heifer with you, and say, 'I have come to sacrifice to the Lord.' Then invite Jesse to the sacrifice, and I will show you what*

> *you shall do; you shall anoint for Me the one I name to you." So Samuel did what the Lord said and went to Bethlehem. And the elders of the town trembled at his coming, and said, "Do you come peaceably?" And he said, "Peaceably; I have come to sacrifice to the Lord. Sanctify yourselves and come with me to the sacrifice." Then he consecrated Jesse and his sons and invited them to the sacrifice. So it was, when they came, that he looked at Eliab and said, "Surely the Lord's anointed is before Him!" But the Lord said to Samuel, "Do not look at his appearance or at his physical stature, because I have refused him. For the Lord does not see as man sees; for man looks at the outward appearance, but the Lord looks at the heart."*

In this chapter and these verses, we see how God led the prophet Samuel to fulfill His will of choosing the next king of Israel. What is amazing to me is how God gave the prophet all of the details. God instructed Samuel on what to do, who to see, where to go, what to bring, who to look for, and what not to look for in His selection for the next king.

As Samuel listened to the voice of God, he went one by one searching for the one who would be anointed with oil and appointed as king in the line of Jesse. Interestingly, Samuel did not second-guess God. He knew God said the next king would be from the house of Jesse. Therefore, in 1 Samuel 16:11-13, we read, *And Samuel said to Jesse, "Are all the young men here?" Then he said, "There remains yet the youngest, and there he is, keeping the sheep."* Samuel was in sync and in line with God and was determined to obey what God told him to do. Continuing with the chapter and verses we read:

> *And Samuel said to Jesse, "Send and bring him. For we will not sit down till he comes here." So he sent and brought him in. Now he was ruddy, with bright eyes, and good-looking. And the Lord said, "Arise, anoint him; for this is the one!" Then Samuel took the horn of oil and anointed him in the midst of his brothers; and the Spirit of the Lord came upon David from that day forward.*

God, not man, made the choice.

Associate riding on the moving train with the opportunity to read your Bible more, though the suggestions are not intended to create any rituals. The purpose is to not limit the places to read and meditate on God's Word and explore the promises in the Bible, but to create an expectation on how God could work inspiration and encouragement in our everyday lives.

I find the story of David fascinating because it reminds me of the power of God, and it does not matter what others think or say about you. All you need to be concerned with is what God says about you. God is still choosing and anointing people to fulfill His purpose. He will send those who will confirm the anointing on your life. Also, God knows the intentions of your heart whether they are good or bad. If it is in your heart to do a good deed and someone tries to twist it around as if it was bad, do not dwell on it. God knows what you intended to do in that situation. I am so glad God looks at us not the way man does!

> *But the* LORD *said to Samuel, "Do not look at his appearance or at his physical stature, because I have* [*refused him. For the* LORD *does not see as man sees; for man looks at the outward appearance, but the* LORD *looks at the heart."* 1 Samuel 16:7

"E" Train

On August 19, 1933, the NYC e train service officially began, running between Roosevelt Avenue – Jackson Heights and the Hudson Terminal (current World Trade Center station). The NYC e train service operates at all times. The normal service pattern for the NYC e train is between Jamaica Center – Parsons/Archer in Jamaica, Queens, and World Trade Center in Lower Manhattan, running express on the IND Queens Boulevard Line in Queens and local in Manhattan.

During late nights, the NYC e train service runs local along its entire route. The NYC e train also serves two local stops in eastern Queens (75th Avenue and Briarwood – Van Wyck Boulevard) on evenings and weekends as you can see in e train map NYC. Limited rush hour service of NYC e train runs fully express to 179th Street at the end of the Queens Boulevard Line in Jamaica.[12]

The E train commute is exciting to me because it is one of the local trains that goes to Queens. This reminds me of Queen Esther. This is another story of basically "rags to riches," where God is orchestrating the story. Here we have Esther, the niece of Mordecai, who was chosen to be queen. She was in the right place at the right time; however, there was a man named Haman who did not like the Jewish people. In fact, in Esther 3:8-9, we read:

> *Then Haman said to King Ahasuerus, "There is a certain people scattered and dispersed among the people in all the provinces of your kingdom; their laws are different from all other people, and they do not keep the king's laws. Therefore, it is not fitting for the king to let them remain. If it pleases the king, let a decree be written that they be destroyed, and I will pay ten thousand talents of silver into the hands of those who do the work, to bring it into the king's treasuries."*

Unbeknownst to King Ahasuerus, his chosen queen was Jewish. As we read in Esther 7:3-6:

Then Queen Esther answered and said, "If I have found favor in your sight, O king, and if it pleases the king, let my life be given me at my petition, and my people at my request. For we have been sold, my people and I, to be destroyed, to be killed, and to be annihilated. Had we been sold as male and female slaves, I would have held my tongue, although the enemy could never compensate for the king's loss." So King Ahasuerus answered and said to Queen Esther, "Who is he, and where is he, who would dare presume in his heart to do such a thing?" And Esther said, "The adversary and enemy is this wicked Haman!"

In this love story, we learn about a man's love for his wife that transcends race, religion, and background. Esther, through the help of God, was able to change the decree that was meant to destroy her and her people. More interesting, we see how God turned what was meant for harm into good, like the circumstances of Joseph's life. Joseph said to his brothers in Genesis 50:20, *But as for you, you meant evil against me; but God meant it for good.* Continuing with

Esther 7:9, we see the tables have turned: *Then the king said, "Hang him on it!" So they hung Haman on the gallows that he had prepared for Mordecai.*

The Book of Esther is one of the books in the Old Testament that starts with the letter "E." There are also wonderful stories in Exodus, Ezra, Ecclesiastes, and Ezekiel that show God's love, mercy, compassion, and grace, as well as His continuing desire to gather His people. In the New Testament, we find Ephesians, a guide to godly living and relationships. All are excellent books in the Bible you could read.

As Ecclesiastes 3:1 reminds us, *To everything there is a season, A time for every purpose under heaven.* And in Esther 4:14, Mordecai's message to Esther is, "Yet who knows whether you have come to the kingdom for such a time as this?" It was a time for Esther to be queen, a time to protect the Jewish people from Haman's hatred, and a time to bring peace.

Yet who knows whether you have come to the kingdom for such a time as this? Esther 4:14

"F" Train

The f train Sixth Avenue Local is a rapid transit service of the New York City Subway. The f train is colored bright orange on route signs, station signs, and the official subway map, since it runs on the IND Sixth Avenue Line through Manhattan ... Peak-direction express service on the f train in Brooklyn began on Monday, Sept. 16, 2019. Express service off train runs between Church Av and Jay St-MetroTech, making one stop at 7 Av. F Express riders can save up to 7 minutes during their morning commute, and up to 6 minutes on their afternoon ride home.[13]

The F train, to me, resonates "faith." Those who are more mature in the faith tend to read the Bible often; however, it seems most of the younger generation is not too concerned about reading the Bible. There are also the non-believers who neglect the Bible as a source of faith. Perhaps this could be one way to get young believers and non-believers more involved in reading the Bible, possibly experiencing an encounter with the Living Word of God and becoming a Christian. We never know who or what God uses or when, where, or how He chooses to draw people to Him. One of our responsibilities as Christians is to lift Him up. Jesus said in John 12:32, *"And I, if I am lifted up from the earth, will draw all peoples to Myself."* I believe lifting Him up could be in psalms, songs, praises, music and instruments, writing, and other creative ways!

The concept is to lift Him up and point others to the cross. Let us not put God in a box. We do the lifting, and He will do the drawing. As the young believers or non-believers become more mature Christians or believers, they will begin building a foundation of faith.

In general, the F train could provide an opportunity to explore the Bible through words that start with "F." Galatians 5:22 tells us that one of the fruits of the Spirit is faithfulness. The Book of Hebrews is often called the book of faith. Also, we are told to live by faith. There are many testimonies of people living by faith. In John 11:25-26, we read, *Jesus said to her [Martha], "I am the resurrection and the life. He who believes in Me, though he may die, he shall live. And whoever lives and believes in Me shall never die. Do you believe this?"* That is what we call faith. Jesus asked Martha, "Do you believe this?" What would be your answer if Jesus asked you the same question?

Fruit of the Spirit Activity

Galatians 5:22-23 states, *But the fruit of the Spirit is love, joy, peace, longsuffering, kindness, goodness, faithfulness, gentleness, self-control.* There are nine fruits of the Spirit, and for each one, rank yourself according to how the fruit or attribute matches you. For example, if love is an attribute, you are most likely to exhibit rank love as nine, and if having kindness is your next best attribute, rank it as eight, and continue this process until you have ranked all nine. After you have completed your ranking, do not share your ranking, but ask someone who is close to you to rank you based on the nine fruits of the Spirit. Again, do not share your ranking. Once he or she is finished, make a comparison. Did the person also rank, for example, love as nine for you? If there is a great discrepancy between how you ranked yourself and how the other person ranked you, just review and ask God what the fruits are that you need to improve in as it relates to the fruit of the Spirit.

In the glossary, you'll find tables listing the fruit of the Spirit, one for ranking yourself and the other for someone else to rank you. For the person you would rank you, make sure this is a person who has known you for years.

> *But the fruit of the Spirit is love, joy, peace, longsuffering, kindness, goodness, faithfulness, gentleness, self-control.*
> Galatians 5:22-23

"G" Train

GG — The GG train ran on today's G line but had no express designation. During the 1939 World's Fair, the GG was renamed the "S Special." In 1985, the GG was no longer, and has had the single-G lettering ever since.[14]

In fact, the G train brings us back to the beginning with the Book of Genesis where it all started. Although there is one other book in the Bible that starts with "G," Galatians, we're going to focus on where it all began. In Genesis 1:1-3, we read, *In the beginning God created the heavens and the earth. The earth was without form, and void; and darkness was on the face of the deep. And the Spirit of God was hovering over the face of the waters. Then God said, 'Let there be light'; and there was light.* Out of the darkness, God spoke and brought light. In the first chapter of Genesis, we read first that God said, "Let there be light," and light happened. He said, "Let the waters gather and separate from the dry land," and it happened. He said, "Bring forth grass," and it happened. He said, "Let there be a light by day and one by night," and it happened, He said, "Let there be living creatures in the waters and birds flying above or in the sky," and it happened. God created every living beast of the air, water, and land, and He ended off by saying, "It was good."

The character and integrity of God is revealed here. This gives us a confirmation that reassures us in our daily lives and personal journey with God. If we have some unanswered prayers or promises from God, just rest assured that if God said it, it will happen in His time. As Numbers 23:19 reminds us, *"God is not a man, that He should lie, nor a son of man, that He should repent. Has He said, and will He not do? Or has He spoken, and will He not make it good?"* Yes, we can trust in God!

God's creation of the heavens and earth took five days, and on the sixth day, He made man. Unlike His other creations, we learn in Genesis 1:26, "Then God said, Let Us make man in Our image." Previously in this chapter, we read that there is no mention of God having any assistance in creating the heavens, earth, and the creatures or animals in the sea, land, or air; however, now we read that when creating man, God solicited the help of others. This unique creation called "man" required the totality of God, which expresses the totality of man. God is a tri-being, with the attributes and traits of God the Father, God the Son, and God the Holy Spirit. According to Genesis 2:7, *And the Lord God formed man of the dust of the ground and breathed into his nostrils the breath of life; and man became a living being.* Notice in the Book of Genesis that the only creation God personally breathed into was a man. Adam was born or created with God's Holy Spirit! It was not until, I believe, God as the Holy Spirit breathed into Adam that the relationship formed between God and man—a bonding took place. The same Spirit in Genesis 1:2, when "the earth was without form, and void; and darkness was on the face of the deep. And the Spirit of God that was hovering over the face of the waters" was somehow now in Adam. It is a mystery. Even John 3:8 states, *The wind blows where it wishes, and you hear it, but cannot tell where it comes from and where it goes. So is everyone who is born of the Spirit.* Adam received this Spirit in the beginning. Although God did not breathe into Eve, I believe since she was made from Adam, she also received God's Holy Spirit because the two became one in the same Spirit.

Today, we have the same privilege to receive God's Holy Spirit through Jesus Christ and be born again. This is a way to form a bond with God and become intimate with the Lord. There are people who have not bonded with God through His Spirit. Jesus said to Nicodemus in John 3:3, "*Most assuredly, I say to you, unless one is born again, he cannot see the kingdom of God... which is born of the Spirit is spirit.*"

If you have not received Jesus Christ as your Lord and Savior, Romans 10:9-13 gives us the way to salvation:

> *"That if you confess with your mouth the Lord Jesus and believe in your heart that God has raised Him from the dead, you will be saved. For the Scripture says, 'Whoever believes on Him will not be put to shame.' For there is no distinction between Jew and Greek, for the same Lord over all is rich to all who call upon Him. For 'whoever calls on the name of the Lord shall be saved.'"*

As mentioned, there is another book in the Bible that begins with "G," which is Galatians, where we are taught about the "fruit of the Spirit." You previously read about the

F train, and if you have not already, you have an assignment to complete: the fruit of the Spirit activity.

This brings us to the next train letter "J," and I am quite sure you know what we will mention in this chapter. If you guessed "Jesus," you are right.

For "whoever calls on the name of the Lord shall be saved."
Romans 10:13

"J" Train

The Jamaica Line or j train then known as the Broadway Elevated–was one of the original elevated lines in Brooklyn, completed in 1893 from Cypress Hills west to Broadway Ferry in Williamsburg.[9] The j train Nassau Street Express and Z Nassau Street Express (earlier Jamaica Express) are two rapid transit services of the B Division of the New York City Subway.[15]

A commute on this train will give you a wonderful opportunity to focus on Jesus. Not to say this is the only time you focus on Him, but rather readjust your train of thought and focus on Jesus while you are riding on this train. What a marvelous time to acknowledge God's goodness, mercy, and forgiveness; a time to recognize what He has done on the cross and what He is currently doing in your life. Through the chaos of the day, the noise of the train, and the crowded platform, you could still find quiet time to reflect on the goodness of the Lord.

Perhaps this is a time you might want to think about the things or people that the Lord saved you from. Another event in history that rocked this nation was 9/11. I cannot believe it happened over twenty-two years ago, yet I can still recall as I exited the train that I could see the plane in one of the World Trade buildings on the right. I walked to the office in disbelief at what I saw, and when I entered the building, I asked one of my coworkers, "What is going on? Are we being attacked?" Then announcements and emails were being sent to the workers while top executives came on the floor to tell us what happened and our next steps. It was so surreal. I remember while on the train coming to the office, there was a young child who did not want to get off the train. The child was screaming at the top of his lungs. This woman, who I think was his mother, was trying to exit the train, but the young child yelled and pulled back, saying, "No, no, I do not want to go!" He kept on screaming and saying these words. It was one of the World Trade Center stops. The woman was able to get the child off of the train, and I watched as she stood on the platform, kneeling before the child to talk to him. I do not know if this was a delay with a purpose. Only God knows, but I do wonder if her delay somehow prevented her and that child from getting into any harm.

Throughout the days, weeks, and months to follow, I heard stories of how people were supposed to be at or near the World Trade Center, but did not go because of reassignments to another building or project, a child was sick, they did not go to work because they were not feeling well, and the list goes on. Was it divine intervention? Was it God ordering their steps? I choose to believe so. Worship, praise, and thank God for His divine protection, mercy, and grace. Reading the Word of God is a privilege, and it's a blessing to learn more about the awesome God who loves us.

In Joshua 1:8, he said, *This Book of the Law shall not depart from your mouth, but you shall meditate in it day and night, that you may observe according to all that is written in it. For then you will make your way prosperous, and then you will have good success.*

As mentioned, the message I would like to convey to you is to explore ways to acknowledge and thank Jesus and to encourage you to spend time reading your Bible. This process I am sharing is not any step-by-step guide or "cookie-cutter" way to experience the Lord, nor is it meant to persuade you into forming any type of ritual or religion. The purpose of this book is to get you into a mindset of reading and meditating on the Word of God and acknowledging Jesus as your Lord and Savior not just on Sundays or in church, but also through your life experiences. As you grow in your awareness and in your relationship with Jesus, let the Lord lead you in all of His ways.

In the meantime, for the young Christian, pick up your Bible and learn more about the life of Jesus Christ in the New Testament. As you also read the Old Testament, see where Jesus presents Himself.

As I recall the song "Not About Us" by Bishop Noel Jones, I am reminded that nothing is about us, but about Jesus.[16]

This Book of the Law shall not depart from your mouth, but you shall meditate in it day and night, that you may observe according to all that is written in it. For then you will make your way prosperous, and then you will have good success.

Joshua 1:8

"L" Train

The NYC l train service, being a local train, was originally the LL. From 1928 to 1967, the same service was assigned the BMT number 16. In 1924, part of the eventual 14th Street - Canarsie Line opened, called the "14th Street - Eastern District Line" (commonly the "14th Street–Eastern Line"), and carried the number 16. This was extended east, and in 1928 the NYC l train was joined to the existing Canarsie Line east of Broadway Junction. Since that time, the 14th Street–Canarsie Line service has operated as it is today, except for an extension from Sixth Avenue to Eighth Avenue, which opened in 1931 to connect to the new Eighth Avenue Subway.[17]

While living in New York, I rode the Canarsie Line, or L train. I experienced God's love for me in an amazing way as I commuted to and from work on this line. It was interesting, and at first, I thought it was just a coincidence;

however, I recall one preacher said, "There are no coincidences with God." With his message of hope, I then began to take notice of what and who I saw, the people, places, and things around me, typical nouns, and when and where I encountered something that seemed different or stood out to me. Could you imagine God answering your prayers on a train? I could not explain it and was hesitant to embrace this new way God was answering my prayers. Nonetheless, I could not ignore it.

As a child, I believe, the church building was the only place to go to hear the Word of God. No one said or preached about this, but I grew up believing that church was the only place to experience the presence of God. As my spiritual eyes and ears were being renewed and awakened, I did not limit God in the walls of this building. Absolutely, God could answer prayers in the church; I am not disputing the place. I am recognizing and experiencing that the omnipresent God is truly omnipresent.

So, rather than dismissing the connection that my prayers were somehow miraculously answered during my everyday activity, I began to recognize that my prayers were answered by God from a word someone said, a subway advertisement, an encounter with someone (perhaps an angel), meeting a friend or neighbor, or reading what was on a shopping bag someone was carrying. As mentioned, I could not explain it, but all I could say was, *Thank you, God, for answering my prayers*. Perhaps the "L" in this train stands for "love." It is a reminder of a scripture verse that we see displayed at football and baseball games or quoted by many preachers that *God so loved the world that He gave His only begotten Son and whoever believes in Him shall not perish but have everlasting life* (John 3:16).

The next incident I am about to share happened during my commute from work on a numbered train. It was the number 6 train, the Lexington Avenue local train. Miracles can happen anywhere, and this one occurred on this train. Since I am not writing about the numbered trains in this book, I will share the miraculous experience on this line because it was the connecting subway line from a lettered train.

When I was coming from a work assignment, as was the norm, I would walk into the subway and get my MetroCard to pay to ride the New York City train. I would walk down the stairs to the platform and stand in the location where the subway car I needed would stop. This location and subway car would be the best place for me to exit the train and connect to the stairs I needed to walk up to transfer to my connecting train. I am mentioning the details because of the nine or ten subway cars for this train, I would enter the second to the last subway car. It was the subway car that I knew would provide the most convenient access to my transfer point.

On this day, I entered the train, found a seat, and sat down. I watched as a vigorous elderly lady entered the train with a beautiful and welcoming smile. I was curious who she was smiling at. It turned out that she was smiling at me as if we knew one another. Since she was smiling so brightly at me, I was trying to figure out where I might have seen her, but this woman did not look familiar to me. In fact, her attire, size, shape, and face reminded me of a woman I saw on a television show. She could have been someone's grandmother. Nevertheless, her intentions were to meet and greet me. She sat next to me on the train, and still smiling, said hi. Since she was an elderly woman and out of respect, I smiled and said hi, as well. She did not just want to say hi, though; she wanted to have a conversation.

The conversation at first was very casual. "How are you doing?" and my reply, "I am doing well, and how are you?" Just casual conversation, and then she went on to talk about marriage and men. What?! If I could or was near the emergency brake, I might have pulled the handle to stop this train. The thought that went through my head was, *Is this really happening?* How did this woman I did not know enter a subway car that I was in and begin to talk about a matter I was talking about with God in my "secret closet or place"? In Matthew 6:6, it tells us, *But you, when you pray, go into your room, and when you have shut your door, pray to your Father who is in the secret place; and your Father who sees in secret will reward you openly.* Only God knew of this prayer; no one else. I did not share my conversation or prayer with anyone. Was this how God was rewarding me "openly"? The "reward" was the answer to my prayer, and the "openly" could not get any more open than on a public train. Only God knows. Might I add that I unknowingly met my future husband on a train. The guy, over thirty years ago, who said hi to me on a New York City Subway train, was later introduced to me by a friend on a "blind date."

Nevertheless, my full attention was now on this elderly woman, and I was curious about what she was going to say next. I tuned in and began to listen. She spoke about men as the head of the household and that they needed to be respected. Yes, I knew this according to Ephesians 5:25-33,

Husbands, love your wives, just as Christ also loved the church ... and let the wife see that she respects her husband. "Definitely," I wanted to say; it also said for husbands to "love your wives," but I did not go there. However, as wives, we need to recognize how our husbands show love. Sometimes, the way they show love is not the way we receive love. Then, in turn, we think they do not love us. Remembering a birthday, anniversary, or other special days and giving a card or a gift is one expression of love. I recall during one of the church conferences, we were taught from Gary Chapman's book on the five love languages, and one woman mentioned that if her husband washes the dishes and does things around the house, that shows her he loves her. Her love language was "acts of kindness."

But I digress.

This elderly woman began to elaborate and, I believe, was sharing her experiences. The words she spoke were nothing I had not heard before, but for some reason, I believe God was using this woman to speak to me. Sometimes, we tend to tune out or ignore people who are close to us when they speak about certain things because we think we know better. Interestingly, I have witnessed people who were told one thing over and over by one person, and when someone else tells them that same exact thing, for some reason, the person receives it as a new revelation, while in fact, you have been told about these many times before. Perhaps I was in this type of mindset and God was sending this one person to get through to me and jar my memory.

Do not get me wrong; I do respect my husband, but in every marriage, you have your better and worse, but for some reason, when she spoke about the issue and what needed to be done, it seemed more like she was teaching me, and as a student, I wanted to learn what she had to say. She began to speak about her experience on this topic and was imparting something in me from her experiences and wisdom. As I grabbed the nuggets of wisdom she spoke, she asked with a smile, "Do you understand?" Okay, this was rather awkward. Now, it was more like a stern rebuke, or she wanted to make sure I understood what she was saying. Not for me to just hear what she was telling me, but to do. Like James 1:22 says, *But be doers of the word, and not hearers only, deceiving yourselves.* Almost like when you reprimand children and ask them if they understood what you said and that you meant business.

As mentioned at that moment in time, she was the teacher and I was the student. I recall how the twelve disciplines called Jesus the "Good Teacher." In John 3:1-2, we read Nicodemus calls Jesus a teacher: *his man [Nicodemus] came to Jesus by night and said to Him, "Rabbi, we know that You are a teacher come from God; for no one can do these signs that You do unless God is with him."*

God was with this lady. After her words, I acknowledged her with a "yes" that I understood what she was telling me and appreciated her words. She then got up and exited the train. She entered and exited the subway car the same way—with a smile. I intentionally watched her as she exited and firmly kept my eyes on her to see if she would miraculously disappear as a man did on a similar learning experience, but she stood there on the train platform, smiling and waving goodbye to me. I waved back in disbelief of what had just happened. It was as if we were old friends. In fact, this elderly woman of wisdom became an inspiration to me. She spoke a word in due season. This experience I will never forget and was one of the experiences that created the title of this book, *Jesus on the Trainline*. I was sharing with God my prayers and my heart's desires, and He miraculously met the needs through people or angels on the train.

I continued to watch her waving as the train entered the tunnel and I could no longer see her. I thought, *God, is this Your way of showing me that You do not just get involved in the big problems, but You are deeply involved in every intricate detail of my life? That I could come to You for anything and everything that matters to me in my life? More amazing, if You could send an angel to help lead and guide me when needed on a train, You could do anything to reach me.* God revealed His love for me through it all. John 3:16 tells us that God loves us!

This is the reason I do not dismiss people who enter my circle because as stated in Hebrews 13:2, *Do not forget to entertain strangers, for by so doing some have unwittingly entertained angels.* If it meets the circumstance you are praying about, listen. There might also be a time that what the person is saying is not relevant at that moment, but do take it to heart and ask God if there is something He wants you to know. Do like Mary when Jesus was a child; she did not dismiss what He was saying, *But Mary kept all these things and pondered them in her heart* (Luke 2:19). Yes, I have noticed that the revelation or words spoken by others might not be for that specific time, but for another time. It is interesting that when an event or circumstance comes around in the future, the words spoken in the past will come to mind, and I would know that it was meant for a future time. Almost like time travel, the word you received in the past is transported in your mind and used for future events or circumstances as you need it in the future. A real-time, present event will trigger what was said in a past event. It was purposed for a set time or future event.

I am so grateful to God for His mercy and grace. All through the years, I did not realize He has been leading me and guiding me. I honestly believe that there is a reason and purpose for everything. Also, I honestly believe there are angels among us. Angels are those who are sent by God with a message. They could also be friends, family members, acquaintances, someone you meet, or supernatural angels in disguise from heaven doing God's will.

But Jesus looked at them and said, "With men it is impossible, but not with God; for with God **all things are possible***."*
Mark 10:27

"M" Train

The m train is the only non-shuttle route that has both of its terminals in the same borough (Queens). The terminals of the m train, Metropolitan Avenue and 71st Avenue, are 2.5 miles apart, marking the shortest geographic distances between termini for a New York City Subway non-shuttle service.[16] The line was officially designated "M" after the Chrystie Street changeover on November 27, 1967, but did not appear on the trains until the transition to rolling stock equipped with appropriate roll signs.[18]

We have signs in life that give us direction, instructions, or information. There are the signs we see while driving (i.e., the traffic stop, yield, and railroad crossing signs). We can discern if it is about to rain when we see signs of dark clouds hovering, and we can see the signs of spring by the budding trees and flowers. We are not to intentionally look for "signs and wonder," but I believe when they do happen, we should discern if they are from God. Usually, these types of miracles confirm or affirm what you already know and point you in a direction that aligns with the Word of God. If anyone or anything leads you away from the gospel, the truth about the true living God, or Jesus Christ, then dismiss it. The Bible is the truth.

We have websites and apps on how to read the Bible in 365 days. Why not have another way of reading the Bible by associating your daily commute or knowledge of trainlines with the books in the Bible?

So, the next time you look at a subway map, you should create your route and think about what to read in the Bible. Just like when we were taught in elementary school that "A is for apple" and "B is for banana," we can associate the A train with the Books of Amos and Acts, or for Adam and Abram, as examples.

Back to the M train and books in the Bible that begin with "M." For example, we have Micah and Malachi in the Old Testament and Matthew and Mark in the New Testament.

During my tenure, working at one of the major publications in corporate America, I had the words from Micah 6:8 on my wall, *He has shown you, O man, what is good; And what does the Lord require of you but to do justly, To love mercy, And to walk humbly with your God?* Throughout the day, I would glance at this scripture. Those who entered my office would also see these words. It was not on display for any other reason but to remind myself of what God expected of me not only in the workplace, but in my everyday life. However, it had the added benefit of others seeing this passage. A word that begins with "M" in this passage is "mercy." The word "mercy" is mentioned 276 times in the Bible.

> *The Hebrew meaning of "mercy" is Rachamim. The sound "cha" in "ra-cha-mim" is pronounced like the Spanish "ja" in the word "jalapeño." "Ra-cha-min" is a noun, but it can also be used as a verb, as it often happens in prayer. When it is a verb, we say "ra-chem" for "have mercy." It is amazing that the emotion "mercy" or "compassion," "ra-cha-min," is derived from the name of the most motherly organ in the human body: the womb, "re-chem." This is where the strongest connection of compassion and love are bonded between the mother and the baby respectively. Men may need to*

> *learn this, but if you are a mother, no further words are necessary; you have experienced this compassion firsthand. "Ra-chem" (give or have mercy) is the imperative form (commanding or requesting something from others). The imperative form is considered an actual tense in Hebrew, in addition to past, present and future.*[19]

Perhaps this could be a time to revisit your response to others if you are exhibiting mercy or compassion with others. I am not leaving myself out of this. As Matthew 5:7 reminds us, "Blessed are the merciful, for they shall obtain mercy."

> *He has shown you, O man, what is good; And what does the Lord require of you But to do justly, To love* **mercy**, *And to walk humbly with your God?* Micah 6:8

"N" Train

The route that is now the n train was originally BMT service 4, known as the Sea Beach Line or Sea Beach Express. On June 22, 1915, the current BMT Sea Beach Line opened, replacing a street level "el" that branched off of the Fifth Avenue El with the former BMT West End Line. Originally, the n train used the south tracks of the Manhattan Bridge, which at that time connected to the BMT Nassau Street Line... The n train service operates at all times between Ditmars Boulevard in Astoria, Queens, and Stillwell Avenue in Coney Island, Brooklyn via Astoria in Queens, the south side of the Manhattan Bridge, and Fourth Avenue and Sea Beach lines in Brooklyn as its shown in n train map. At all times except late nights, the n train operates express along Fourth Avenue, bypassing DeKalb Avenue, and local elsewhere. During late nights, it makes all stops along its entire route and uses the Montague Street Tunnel to travel between Manhattan and Brooklyn to replace the R.[20]

There are only three books in the Bible that begin with the letter "N." They are in the Old Testament: Numbers, Nehemiah, and Nahum. I have read Numbers and Nehemiah often, but Nahum I have not really meditated on. In general, if there is a book in the Bible that you have not explored, perhaps this could be the opportunity to read it. In fact, while asking God which book of the three that began with "N" should I reference for this section, Nahum came to mind. In this three-chapter book, the first chapter begins with describing God as a "jealous and avenging God."

We read in the Bible that God is a jealous God and does not want us to worship, praise, or give accolades to any other god. In Exodus 20, we are introduced to God's commandments, and in verses 4-6, it reads:

> *You shall not make for yourself a carved image—any likeness of anything that is in heaven above, or that is in the earth beneath, or that is in the water under the earth; you shall not bow down to them nor serve them. For I, the Lord your God, am a jealous God,*

> *visiting the iniquity of the fathers upon the children to the third and fourth generations of those who hate Me, but showing will mercy to thousands, to those who love Me and keep My commandments.*

Basically, we are not to create and worship any idols. God created everything, and all credit goes to Him. It is disrespectful to give credit to someone else for another person's work. For example, you baked a cake and put all of your energy and resources into that cake, you took the time to go and get the ingredients, you measured and mixed all the ingredients and placed the mixture in the pans, and also, you set the oven to the right temperature to bake the cake. You waited until it was golden brown on top and waited until it was cool. Then carefully removed the cake from the pan. To make it more of a masterpiece, you decided to make homemade frosting instead of using store-bought frosting. All of the ingredients were made from scratch. Perhaps you decorated it to make it more presentable. As you slice the cake for others to eat, you hear someone else getting credit for what you have done. Would you like someone else to take the credit for the cake you made? I believe this is like what

God is telling us. He deserves all of the honor and praise. For He is the only God who created the heavens and the earth and all that is within.

As mentioned, another attribute Nahum describes God as is avenging. We see in 2 Samuel 22:48 and Psalm 18:47 that "it is God who avenges me, and subdues the peoples under me." The previous sentence is worth emphasizing and remembering. God is our vindicator. It is God, not us, who avenges. As mentioned in Deuteronomy 32:35, Romans 12:19, and Hebrews 10:30, God said, "Vengeance is Mine."

This is to say, vengeance or revenge is not an attribute that Christians should display. Yes, there are hurtful people and circumstances that call for retaliation, but this is not the godly way to handle them. We are to give these hurts over to God. Let Him handle them. We take on the responsibilities God has given us to do, and if God said, "This is mine," that means leave it to Him. Also, do not get vengeance and a person's choice confused. God has given people the right to choose, and for example, someone not attending your event is their choice. Do not assume it was revenge.

"Q" Train

The Q train was introduced as a service identifier for the Brighton Beach Express via Broadway (Manhattan) on the rollsigns of the R27 class of subway cars as they were delivered beginning in 1960 and on all subsequent equipment ordered for the IND/BMT divisions of the New York City subway system ... Current plans for the Second Avenue Subway provide for the q train to be extended northward from 57th Street via the BMT 63rd Street Line, which is currently used only during service disruptions as its shown in q train map. The q train would stop at Lexington Avenue – 63rd Street at the currently-hidden northern side of the platforms to provide a cross-platform interchange to the IND 63rd Street Line (currently served by the F train).[21]

There are no books in the Bible that begin with the letter "Q." However, perhaps this is a time to learn more about the queens mentioned in the Bible. Earlier, we pointed out Esther, who became queen, and through the help of God, saved the Jewish people. Then there is Esther's predecessor, Queen Vashti, who defied the king. Also, in the Old Testament, there is the Queen of Sheba.

> *Now when the queen of Sheba heard of the fame of Solomon, she came to Jerusalem to test Solomon with hard questions ... So Solomon answered all her questions; there was nothing so difficult for Solomon that he could not explain it to her. And when the queen of Sheba had seen the wisdom of Solomon, the house that he had built ... his entryway by which he went up to the house of the Lord, there was no more spirit in her. Then she said to the king: "It was a true report which I heard in my own land about your words and your wisdom. However I did not believe their words until I came and saw with my own eyes; and indeed, the half of the greatness of your wisdom was not told me. You exceed the fame of which I heard. Happy are your men and happy are these your servants, who stand continually before you and*

> *hear your wisdom! Blessed be the Lord your God, who delighted in you, setting you on His throne to be king for the Lord your God!"* 2 Chronicles 9:1

Not only did the Queen of Sheba acknowledge King Solomon's wisdom, she also acknowledged and blessed God.

There is mention of another queen in the Bible, Queen Candace, the queen of the Ethiopians (Acts 8:27). For those who are history buffs, this could be the opportunity to learn more about Queen Candace and other queens in the Bible.

In general, according to 1 Peter 2:9-10, we are royalty—the people of God. It states, *But you are a chosen generation, a royal priesthood, a holy nation, His own special people, that you may proclaim the praises of Him who called you out of darkness into His marvelous light; who once were not a people but are now the people of God, who had not obtained mercy but now have obtained mercy.*

"R" Train

In March 1905, the route of the modern R train was finally laid out: "an independent subway line through Fourth avenue from Old Slip, Manhattan, through Montague street to Court street, to Atlantic avenue, to Fourth avenue," as the Eagle reported.[22]

The r train subway is the longest New York City Subway service without an elevated section, although there is a small opening between 59th Street and Bay Ridge Avenue in Brooklyn when the Fourth Avenue Line passes over a valley containing the Long Island Rail Road Bay Ridge Branch tracks.[23]

There is one book beginning with the letter "R" in the Old Testament, and that is Ruth. In the New Testament, there are two—Romans and Revelations.

I find the Book of Ruth fascinating because of how Naomi guided Ruth to find her future husband. Ruth followed the detailed instructions of Naomi and informed her of all that should take place. How did Naomi know these intricate details and create a plan with specific ways for Ruth to pursue Boaz? From informing Ruth of how to prepare herself, what to wear, where to go, what to do, and telling Ruth to "sit still" (Ruth 3:18) to see if or when Boaz would follow through, the details were more than clever; there was a divine influence that motivated Naomi: "A significant theological point emerges here… Naomi's plan carries out something … understood to be in Yahweh's province."[24] Naomi perhaps was saying, "I will follow Your way, Yahweh, when instructing Ruth on what to do." What an awesome revelation! That leads me to the Book of Revelations.

Often referred to as the "end times book," I must admit, when I was younger, I was apprehensive of reading this book because of the symbolic words and images. I did not understand the symbolism. Later as I read Revelations, I realized the symbolic language of this book was teaching us not to fall prey to sin. The sins in the Church are revealed, and there is a call to repentance. More importantly, it is pointing us to Jesus and His second coming; how an imperfect world needs a perfect savior. Jesus first came as a lamb, but He is coming back as a mighty warrior who will rule the nations and eliminate sin. According to Revelations 19:15-16:

Now out of His mouth goes a sharp sword, that with it He should strike the nations. And He Himself will rule them with a rod of iron. He Himself treads the winepress of the fierceness and wrath of Almighty God. And He has on His robe and on His thigh a name written: KING OF KINGS AND LORD OF LORDS.

We know Jesus, our Savior, but to have Him as Lord over everything is different. It is letting God rule and reign in our lives; to do like Naomi, let God lead. I have been aware of the things that prevent us from living a life dedicated to God. We all have our habits and some things we have inherited. They are known as *generational curses*. At first, I thought they were not real. I heard of things being passed down from one generation to another, but I was naïve to believe in curses. Generational curses are real, and if God did not reveal some stuff, I would think that this was some nonsense and something only ignorant people believed in. None of us are immune from them, and we just need to ask God to reveal them (or perhaps you already know what they are) and bring healing.

I prayed that any would not continue in my generation and the generation after. We need to repent of generational curses from our mother and father's side. At first, I thought it was something that would go away on its own, and that is what the Devil wants us to believe. I noticed how we make excuses for other people's actions and say, "They can't help it; it's in their DNA." However, that DNA could be described as the **D**evil's **N**oticeable **A**ccess in a generation or someone's life. Recognize the DNA in your family. Ask God, "How did it get there?" and "Who allowed the access?" When God gives you the knowledge, ask God what He would want you to do next. It could involve repenting by asking God for forgiveness of what was allowed and asking for a minister's help or deliverance.

We are born in sin, but the good news is Jesus came to set us free from sin. According to 1 John 3:9 (AMP):

> *No one who is born of God [deliberately, knowingly, and habitually] practices sin, because God's seed [His principle of life, the essence of His righteous character] remains [permanently] in him [who is born again—who is reborn from above—spiritually transformed,*

renewed, and set apart for His purpose]; and he [who is born again] cannot habitually [live a life characterized by] sin, because he is born of God and longs to please Him.

Jesus becomes Lord of your life when you are born again.

And He has on His robe and on His thigh a name written: KING OF KINGS AND LORD OF LORDS. Revelations 19:16

"S" Train

In New York City the "S" train is known as the "shuttle." ... there are three dedicated shuttle services on the system: one in Brooklyn, one in Queens, and one in Manhattan... The Brooklyn service is the Franklin Avenue Shuttle. This line links about two miles between Prospect Park and Franklin Avenue ... Once part of a late 1800s railroad, this shuttle was truncated in 1963 ... The Queens shuttle is important, linking a stop on Broad Channel to Rockaway Park, two whole miles being covered with only five stops. This shuttle has been in operation since 1956 and connects some of the farthest-flung communities in the city to the rest of the system ... In terms of the shortest shuttle ride—and the most famous—there is the 42nd Street Shuttle ... Originally part of the IRT subway line, the 42nd Street Shuttle was configured in 1918 and has kept its form since then.[25]

As we refer to the books in the Bible that begin with the letter "S," there are only three, and they can be found in the Old Testament—1 and 2 Samuel and Song of Songs, or Songs of Solomon. Unlike the other books of the Bible, the Songs of Solomon has all the makings of a romantic novel or poetry. It reveals the true love of a man and woman or bride groom and his bride. It has been said this book symbolically shows the love Christ has for His Church.

The Song of Solomon is a lyrical poem that celebrates marital love. Through beautiful sensory scenes and sensual imagery, it provides us with God's wisdom on sexual intimacy ...This Song tells us what God values: a loving marriage, fidelity to another, protection of another, and the valuing of another ... Through the centuries various allegorical interpretations of the Song of Solomon have sought to identify the groom as Christ and the bride as the church (or the groom as God and the bride as Israel).[26]

We read in Revelations 21:9 that the bride is referred to the Lamb's wife: "Come, I will show you the bride, the Lamb's wife." The bride is the Church, and the Lamb of God is Jesus Christ.

The union between man and woman, what we call marriage, is a sacred bond. A covenant relationship has been formed between man, woman, and God. I often say that marriage is not something you take lightly. It is symbolic and should only be entered in with the sanction of God: *So, they are no longer two, but one flesh. Therefore, what God has joined together, let no one separate* (Matt. 19:6 NIV). I often wonder how a couple knows if God joined them together. I think there are two biblically-based truths on how a man or God joins a couple together.

One way is through an introduction. According to Genesis 2:22, *Then the rib which the Lord God had taken from man He made into a woman, and* **He brought her to the man.** I bolded the last five words to emphasize that God introduced Eve to Adam. Also, I believe that God can inspire a person to introduce a woman to her future husband.

The second way is, *He who finds a wife finds a good thing, And obtains favor from the Lord* (Prov. 18:22). Here, I believe, there is something unique and different from a woman looking for a husband versus a man finding his wife. I often hear some women say they are going to find themselves a husband in the church. According to the Bible, it is not the woman seeking a husband; it is the man who finds his wife. To the Holy Spirit-led, godly women, maybe you should reconsider some of those introductions by family members or friends who want to introduce you to a real man. To the Holy Spirit-led, godly men who are reading this book, perhaps the next time you're on a train, you might find your wife.

Come, I will show you the bride, the Lamb's wife.
Revelations 21:9

"W" Train

The MTA w train was introduced on July 22, 2001 when the Manhattan Bridge north tracks were closed for reconstruction... On March 24, 2010 the Metropolitan Transportation Authority (MTA) announced the elimination of the MTA w train due to financial shortfalls with the N and Q replacing it. The MTA w train service ceased operation on June 25, 2010 with the last train bound for Astoria – Ditmars Boulevard leaving Whitehall Street ..." However, "the W train has returned to New York City's subway system after a six-year [November 7, 2015] hiatus.[27]

Like other lettered trains (i.e., the Q train), there are no books in the Bible that begin with the letter "W." However, we can go to Proverbs, which is called the book of wisdom. Proverbs is one book in the Bible that has a wealth of wisdom. Since after six years the W train returned, let's read the "six things" the Lord hates in Proverbs 6:16-19. *These six things the Lord hates, Yes, seven are an abomination to Him: A proud look, A lying tongue, Hands that shed innocent blood, A heart that devises wicked plans, Feet that are swift in running to evil, A false witness who speaks lies, And one who sows discord among brethren.* Although God loves us, He hates sin. Our actions and behavior *do* matter to God. I often wonder if we genuinely believe God is omnipresent, would be mindful of the things we say or do. Also, if we knew that grace was not a license to sin, would we continue sinning? I heard one minister say (I am paraphrasing) that we often say "WWJD," or "What would Jesus do?" But perhaps we should have the mindset of "WWJND," or "What would Jesus *not* do?"

Nonetheless, there are thirty-one proverbs which coincide with the days of the month. Is it a coincidence that we have a proverb for each day? Did God provide us with a daily planner with instructions on topics or subjects to focus on each day? There is a lot of wisdom and understanding, as well as advice, provided to us daily. This understanding could relate to what is happening in your life right now and give you "know-how" on how to conduct yourself, conduct a business, deal with obstacles, relate to others, etc.

For those who might not know, the author of Proverbs is King Solomon, son of King David and Bathsheba. He was born approximately 1030 B.C. and was the tenth son of King David and the second son of Bathsheba. Solomon was the third king, after David and Saul; however, he became the first king of Israel born to a reigning king, and the last king of the United Kingdom of Israel—the ruler of all twelve tribes of Israel.[28]

God gave King Solomon ultimate wisdom. I find Proverbs 3:5-6 comforting and reassuring. When I find that I do not know what to do, I trust that God will lead me. I do not have the answer, but I know my heavenly Father does. All I am to do is trust in Him.

During your everyday commute or in your quiet time, meditate on the Word of the wisest King of all time. As previously mentioned, the Queen of Sheba was in awe of His wisdom, and she gave God glory. Overall, if you do not know what to do, God will direct you into all truth.

Trust in the Lord *with all your heart,*
And lean not on your own understanding; In all your ways acknowledge Him,
And He shall direct your paths. Proverbs 3:5-6

"Z" Train

As we almost come to the end of suggestions or opportunities to read the Bible more by thinking about the letter of trains in New York City and correlating them with some book or topic in the Bible, this brings us to the Z train:

"On December 11th, 1988, Z service was introduced. This line ran skip-stop service in Brooklyn and Queens and skipped Bowery in Manhattan. ... Z Nassau Street Express (earlier Jamaica Express) ... the Z only operates during rush hours in the peak direction; both services use the entire BMT Archer Avenue Line and BMT Jamaica Line from Jamaica Center – Parsons/Archer over the Williamsburg Bridge to Lower Manhattan."[29] Looking back at the "J" line, we see that the "J" and "Z" trains run on the same track.

The Bible has two books that begin with the letter "Z." They are Zephaniah and Zechariah. Let us focus on the Book of Zechariah. It begins with a call to repentance:

> *In the eighth month of the second year of Darius, the word of the Lord came to Zechariah the son of Berechiah, the son of Iddo the prophet, saying, "The Lord has been very angry with your fathers. Therefore say to them, 'Thus says the Lord of hosts: "Return to Me," says the Lord of hosts, "and I will return to you," says the Lord of hosts. "Do not be like your fathers, to whom the former prophets preached, saying, 'Thus says the Lord of hosts: "Turn now from your evil ways and your evil deeds."* Zechariah 1:1-4

As John the Baptist cried out in the wilderness, "Repent, for the kingdom of heaven is at hand!" I believe there is a cry out for repentance in this nation. A repentance of not only what we have done but a repentance of the sins of our forefathers. As mentioned earlier in Exodus 20:5-6, we learned that, *For I, the Lord your God, am a jealous God, [did you know that He is] visiting the iniquity of the fathers upon the children to the third and fourth generations of those who hate Me, but [aren't you glad He is] showing mercy to thousands, to those who love Me and keep My commandments.*

Thank you, Jesus, for Your mercy and grace. Thank God for God-fearing families in this nation!

I could not end this chapter without asking those who have not accepted Jesus Christ as their Lord and Savior to view this as an invitation to know Christ. From A to Z, the Bible tells us in Revelations 21:6 that He is the Alpha and Omega, the first and the last. Jesus said in John 14:6, *"I am the way, the truth, and the life. No one comes to the Father except through Me."* Also, according to Romans 10:9, *That if you confess with your mouth the Lord Jesus and believe in your heart that God has raised Him from the dead, you will be saved.* It's a matter of confessing and believing in Jesus Christ. As you become a new creation in Christ, find a church home, a place where you can grow in the knowledge, wisdom, and understanding of Jesus Christ. A church home that preaches and teaches that Jesus is Lord and Savior. We know that Jesus is our Savior; however, the same emphasis on proclaiming, teaching, and preaching Him as Savior should be on His Lordship. What does it mean to have Jesus as not only our Savior, but also our Lord? To make Jesus Lord over our lives involves making conscious effort to obey God and do the things that pleases God. No, we are not perfect, but we ask God to help us in our weakness. If we ask Him, He will help.

Jesus on the Trainline

Considering all of the unlikely places to meet God, the New York City subway revealed God to me in the most remarkable ways how He intervenes in everyday life. It truly taught me to not limit how God will speak. God answered me in the most unexpected place and used unexpected people to speak to my circumstances. He knew where I was, what I needed, where I was going, and how to get my attention. Why would I think otherwise since God is omnipresent and obviously knew what train I would be riding on my commute back and forth to work?

Should it have been a surprise to me that God could meet my needs in an unexpected place? My experiences were exclusive to me. Nonetheless, whether you associate the train you're commuting on with a story in the Bible, it's up to you. I would, however, like to challenge you to read your Bible more and see how God might meet you!

Let us not put God in a box. I am sharing my train experiences not to get you to take a train to find Jesus; that is not the purpose of the book. This book is to get you into a mindset of knowing that God can show up in unlikely places. *Jesus on the Trainline* is also a reminder to not only go to church, but to read your Bible, as Joshua tells us to meditate on it day and night.

> *This Book of the Law shall not depart from your mouth, but you shall meditate in it day and night, that you may observe to do according to all that is written in it. For then you will make your way prosperous, and then you will have good success.* Joshua 1:8

May the Lord bless you and you seek His face!

Endnotes

1. https://www.youtube.com/watch?v=p6yQzQcolnA.

2. Weir, B. (2015). Vessels of Honor: Predestined for Greatness. Xulon Press.

3. https://www.youtube.com/watch?v=9-UdwlHSyqo

4. Jacob, S. (2022, October 28). Number 17 Meaning in The Bible and Its Significance To Us. Biblekeeper.com. https://www.biblekeeper.com/number-17-meaning-in-the-bible/

5. https://www.introducingnewyork.com/subway

6. https://time.com/3534565/new-york-city-subway-history/

7. Facts about New York City subways and buses. https://new.mta.info/agency/new-york-city-transit/subway-bus-facts-2019

8. https://www.americancityandcounty.com/2020/05/07/new-york-city-subway-deliberately-shut-down-for-the-first-time-in-its-history/

9. https://untappedcities.com/2021/07/06/end-of-a-train-guide/

10. https://www.nycsubway.org/wiki/Subway_FAQ

11. https://maps-nyc.com/maps-new-york-city—-nyc-rail/d-train-map

12. E train map NYC–MTA e train map (New York–USA) (maps-nyc.com)

13. https://maps-nyc.com/maps-new-york-city—-nyc-rail/f-train-map

14. https://untappedcities.com/2013/09/27/cities-101-double-lettered-trains-nyc-subway-system/

15. https://maps-nyc.com/maps-new-york-city—-nyc-rail/j-train-map

16. https://www.youtube.com/watch?v=qn4y1jEM5Fg

17. https://maps-nyc.com/maps-new-york-city—-nyc-rail/l-train-map-nyc

18. M (New York City Subway service)–Alchetron, the free social encyclopedia

19. https://hebrew.jerusalemprayerteam.org/mercy-compassion-womb/

20. https://maps-nyc.com/maps-new-york-city—-nyc-rail/n-train-map

21. https://maps-nyc.com/maps-new-york-city—-nyc-rail/q-train-map

22. https://www.heyridge.com/2016/01/crappy-100th-birthday-bay-ridge-subway/#:~:text=Ups%20and%20Downs%3A%20the%20Spring,%2C%E2%80%9D%20as%20the%20Eagle%20reported.

23. https://maps-nyc.com/maps-new-york-city—-nyc-rail/r-train-subway-map

24. Hubbard, Rubert L., The Book of Ruth, Wm. B. Eerdmans Publishing Co (1959).

25. https://sightsbysam.com/subway-shuttles-new-york-city/#:~:text=While%20many%20of%20the%20regular,Queens%2C%20and%20one%20in%20Manhattan.

26. https://www.crossway.org/articles/the-gospel-in-song-of-solomon/

27. https://abc7ny.com/subway-w-train-mass-transit-serve/1593860/

28. Weir, B. (2015). Vessels of Honor: Predestined for Greatness. Xulon Press.

29. https://mtanyctransitfanon.fandom.com/wiki/BMT_Nassau_Street_Line_(mtamaster_edition)#:~:text=On%20December%2011th%2C%201988%2C%20Z,Nassau%20Street%20service%20in%20Manhattan

Glossary

Fruit of the Spirit (My Ranking) – Pray about it and be honest with yourself. Here is where you could ask the Holy Spirit of God to help you with the ranking.

Fruit of the Spirit	My Ranking
Love	
Joy	
Peace	
Perseverance	
Kindness	
Goodness	
Faithfulness	
Gentleness	
Self Control	

Fruit of the Spirit (Someone Else Ranking You) – If you are married, this is a great opportunity for your spouse to do the ranking. Do not dispute or ask why the person did or did not rank a certain way. After you receive the ranking, make your comparisons. It could be very interesting to know how you rank yourself versus someone else's ranking. As mentioned, do not dispute the other person's ranking. Pray and ask the Holy Spirit about the person's ranking and if there are any necessary changes you need to make or need help in making or improving in a specific "fruit" or trait.

Fruit of the Spirit	Someone Else Ranking
Love	
Joy	
Peace	
Perseverance	
Kindness	
Goodness	
Faithfulness	
Gentleness	
Self Control	

What is interesting is I can often tell the "fruit" of the Spirit God is working or pruning in me. You could recognize it, as well, by the circumstances of situations that tend to come up. In my book *Vessels of Honor: Predestined for Greatness*, it describes and gives examples of what "fruit" God might be working on in you.

For we are His workmanship, created in Christ Jesus for good works, which God prepared beforehand that we should walk in them. Ephesians 2:10

Printed in the USA
CPSIA information can be obtained
at www.ICGtesting.com
LVHW040835220124
769342LV00004B/11